MEDICINAL HERBS IN THE MANAGEMENT OF SKIN DISEASES- AN ETHNO BOTANICAL APPROACH

PROF. DR. RAMASUBRAMANIA RAJA R

Copyright © Prof. Dr. Ramasubramania Raja R
All Rights Reserved.

This book has been published with all efforts taken to make the material error-free after the consent of the author. However, the author and the publisher do not assume and hereby disclaim any liability to any party for any loss, damage, or disruption caused by errors or omissions, whether such errors or omissions result from negligence, accident, or any other cause.

While every effort has been made to avoid any mistake or omission, this publication is being sold on the condition and understanding that neither the author nor the publishers or printers would be liable in any manner to any person by reason of any mistake or omission in this publication or for any action taken or omitted to be taken or advice rendered or accepted on the basis of this work. For any defect in printing or binding the publishers will be liable only to replace the defective copy by another copy of this work then available.

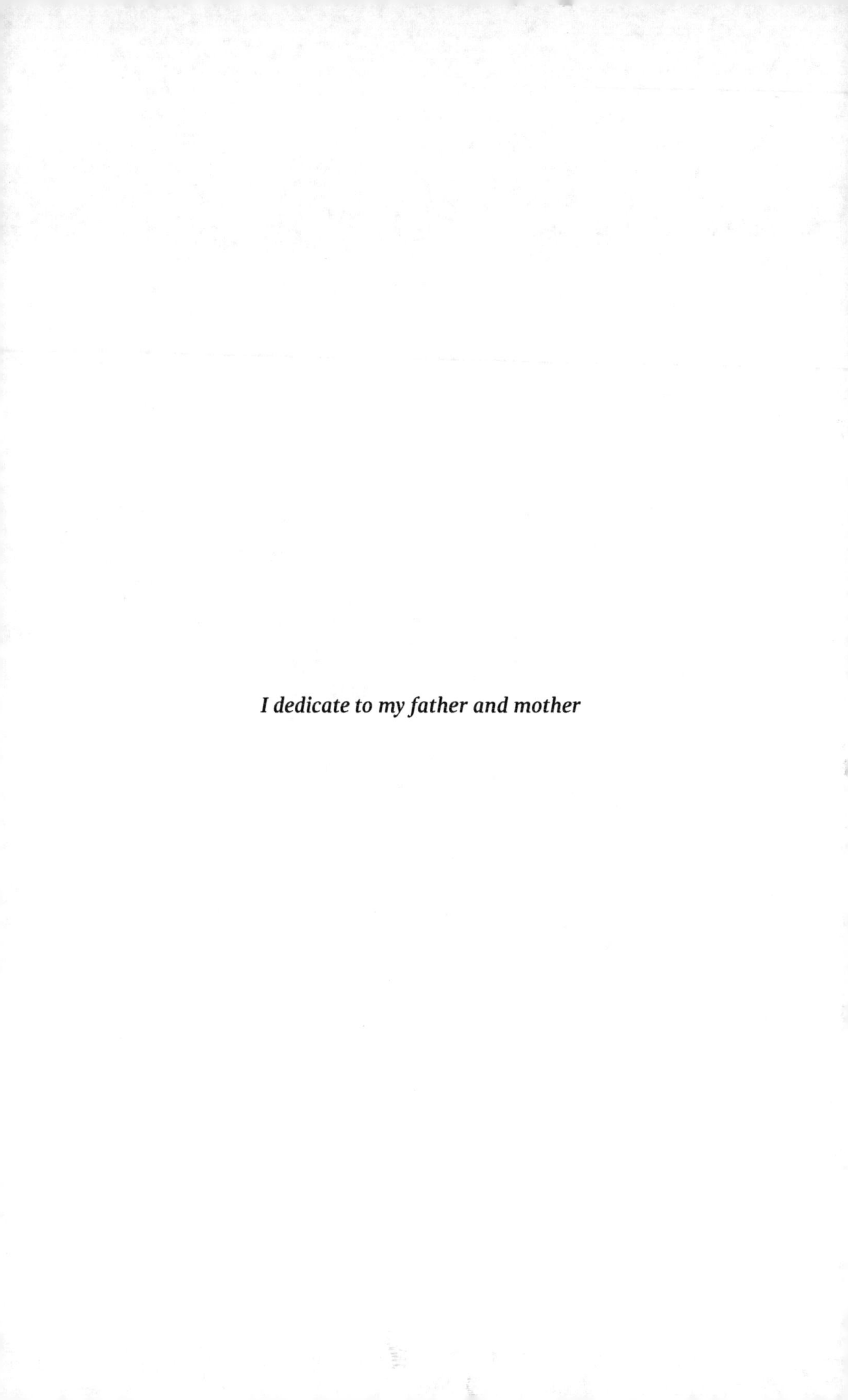

I dedicate to my father and mother

Contents

Foreword

Medicinal herbs in the management of skin diseases an ethno botanical approach is very useful for common peoples those who are interest for the herbals day today activities used.

Skin diseases is a contagious one, it is easily spread one person to another one person by touching, air, water etc.,

The contagious disease is cure by common available herbal drugs only, that herbals here listed and elloporately discussed by author.

Normally the skin diseases are not easily cure and take the medicine very prolong period of time, so the long duration of the time herbal medicine is benefit without any side effects.

i congrats to author here mentioned easy method of appraoches to discuss the several herbs details for cure the skin infection

-Dr.K.Harinadha Baba

Preface

It gives me a great happiness in introducing this book on Pharmacy graduate students.

This book is broadly used in Pharmacy colleges and other institutions all over the world.

The text covers various aspects of investigational techniques about the skin diseases.

We have conceptualized the book in order to bring out the clarity on the practical aspects of the subject, which will help to improve the medicinal herbs basic concept to the students.

Author will welcome helpful suggestions in improvement of this book. The author is hopeful that the book will fulfil the expectations of degree students of B.Pharm and Pharm.D.

Acknowledgements

While a completed book bears the single name of the author, the process that leads to its completion is always accomplished in combination with the dedicated work of other people. I wish to acknowledge my appreciation to certain people.

First and foremost, praises and thanks to the God, the almighty, for this showers of blessings throughout my dissertation work to complete it successfully.

I would like to thank Dr.Y.Hari Babu M.Pharm,Ph.D., Professor cum Principal for providing me his in valuable guidance throughout this entire work. His dynamism, vision, sincerely and motivation have deeply inspired me. I would also like to thank Dr.C.I.Sajeeth M.Pharm,Ph.D., Professor cum Vice Principal, for his constant support which has inspired me throughout the entire work.

I am grateful thanks to my teacher Dr.N.Ravichandran, for their timely advice.

It is my great to acknowledge my deep sense of gratitude to Dr.P.Brihdha Dean, Department of CARISM, SASTRA University, Thanjavur.

I wish to express my heart full thanks to my beloved my mother Mrs.R.Dhanalakshmi, my father late. R.Raja gopal (Retired teacher) my brother Mr.R.Balaji B.Com., and my wife R.Usha B.E., and my daughter R.Likitha and all my friends for their help, encouragement and support during the entire course.

Prologue

We have conceptualized the book in order to bring out the clarity on the practical aspects of the subject, which will help to improve the medicinal herbs basic concept to the students.

Author will welcome helpful suggestions in improvement of this book. The author is hopeful that the book will fulfil the expectations of degree students of Pharm.D.

CHAPTER I

1.0 Introduction:

1. 1 Structure and function of the skin

The skin is the largest organ of the human body, both in terms of surface area and weight. It accounts for 15% of total body weight. It serves as an important environmental interface providing a protective envelope that is crucial for homeostasis. On the other hand, the skin is a major target for toxic insult by a broad spectrum of physical (UV radiation) and chemical (xenobiotic) agents that are capable of altering its structure and function [1]. Skin acts as a physical barrier and prevents harmful substances and microorganisms from entering the body. It protects body tissues and the network of muscles, bones, nerves and blood vessels against injury. It also controls the loss of fluids like blood and water, helps regulate body temperature through perspiration, and protects from the sun's damaging ultraviolet rays. The skin consists of three layers. The epidermis or outer layer is made up of mostly dead cells with a protein called keratin. This makes the layer waterproof and is responsible for protection against the environment. The dermis or middle layer is made up of living cells. It also has blood vessels and nerves that run through it and is primarily responsible for structure and support. The subcutaneous fat layer is primarily responsible for insulation and shock absorbency. It also contains structure like sweat glands, sebaceous glands, hair and hair follicles. Sebaceous glands secrete an oily substance called sebum and are found over the entire surface of the body except for the palms, soles and dorsum of the feet. Sebum protects hair and skin, and keeps them from becoming dry, brittle, and cracked. It also inhibits the growth of microorganisms on skin.

CHAPTER II

1.2. Diseases of the skin

Infectious diseases, particularly skin and mucosal infections, are common in most of the tribal inhabitants due to lack of sanitation, potable water and awareness of hygienic food habits. (2) It has been estimated that skin diseases account for 34% of all occupational diseases. As the primary interface between the body and external environment, the skin provides the first line of defense against broad injury by microbial and chemical agents. And many more factors other than trauma and primary skin disease have been identified as contributory to skin infections and these include immune deficiency diseases, diabetes mellitus and systemic or topical use of steroids [3]. The most damaging consequence of disruption to the skin is invasion by pathogenic microorganisms [4]. Skin diseases can be caused by a variety of the microbes and the skin is a haven for many microbes. In skin and soft tissue infections, the commonest bacterial agents are *Staphylococcus aureus, Streptococcus pyogenes* (Group A haemolytic streptococcus), *Clostridium perfringes* and the bacteriodes group. Others are *Mycobacterium tuberculosis, Mycobacterium leprae, Neisseria gonorrhea, Pasturella tulurensis, Bacillus antracis* and *Pseudomonas aeruginosa.* The common fungi which cause skin infections are *Candida albicans, Candida neoformans, Epidermophyton flocossum, Trychophyton tonsurans, Melassezia furfur,* etc. A broad panel of microbial pathogens are associated with various skin infections. The Gram positive Staphylococci and Streptococci are causing wound infections, furuncles, curbuncles, abscesses, impetigo and erysipelas. The Gram positive Corynebacteria are part of the physiological skin flora. However, Corynebacteria may cause opportunistic skin infections in immunosuppressed patients. The Gram negative *Escherichia coli* are part of the physiological intestinal flora. However, outside the intestine they may cause wound infection and sepsis. Anaerobic Gram negative rods may cause skin infections under certain circumstances, i.e. in immune compromised subjects. The yeast *Candida albicans* and *Candida krusei* may occur in low frequency on skin and mucous membranes without causing symptoms. As opportunistic pathogens they may overgrow the normal flora and cause skin diseases like impetigo and candidiasis in diabetics, adipose and immune deficient subjects [5]. Pseudomonas, Gram negative rod is a frequent pathogen of wound infections. *Pseudomonas aeruginosa* is the most prevalent burn patient's pathogen capable of causing life-threatening illnesses [6]. This bacterium can cause clinically significant infections such as wound and burns infections, giving rise to blue-green pus [7]. Some infections like hot tub folliculitis or nail infection may be mild but others can be fatal without prompt treatment [8]. *Pseudomonas aeruginosa* is able to infect different parts of the body. Several factors like the ability to stick on the cells, minimal food requirements, resistance to many antibiotics, production of proteins that damage tissue, protective outer coat make it a strong opponent. Some diseases caused by fungi include candidiasis, ringworms, athlete's foot, tinea pedis, sporotrichosis, blastomycosis and others not with distinctly specified conditions.

CHAPTER III

1.3 Modes of transmission

Infectious agents may be transmitted either through direct or indirect contact. Direct contact occurs when an individual is infected by contact with the reservoir, for example, by touching an infected person, ingesting infected meat, or bitten by an infected animal or insect. Transmission by direct contact also includes inhaling the infectious agent in droplets emitted by sneezing or coughing and contracting the infectious agent through intimate sexual contact. Indirect contact occurs when a pathogen can withstand the environment outside its host for a long period of time before infecting another individual. Inanimate objects that are contaminated by direct contact with the reservoir may be the indirect contact for a susceptible individual. Ingesting food and beverages contaminated by contact with a disease reservoir is another example of disease transmission by indirect contact.

1.4. Natural drug therapy for microbial skin diseases

The search for newer source of antibiotics is a global challenge preoccupying research institutions, pharmaceutical companies and academia, since many infectious agents are becoming resistant to synthetic drugs [9]. One way to prevent antibiotic resistance of pathogenic species is by using new compounds that are not based on existing synthetic antimicrobial agents. Problem of resistance, environmental degradation and pollution associated with irrational use of orthodox medicines have necessitated renewed interest in nature as a source of effective and safer alternatives in the management of human infections [10]. During the last decade the pace of development of new antimicrobial drugs has slow down while the prevalence of resistance has increase astronomically. In developing countries, the World Health Organization (WHO) estimates that about three quarters of the populations relies on plant based preparations used in their traditional medicinal system and as the basic needs for human primary health care. Plants produce a diverse range of bioactive molecules, making them rich sources of different types of medicine [11]. Natural products, either as pure compounds or as standardized plant extracts, provide unmatched availability of chemical diversity [12]. Several plants containing volatile oils, polyphenols and alkaloids as active constituents are utilized as popular folk medicines, while others gained popularity in the form of finished products collectively named phytomedicines [13]. Plants have always been the principal form of medicine throughout the world, as people strive to stay healthy in the face of chronic stress and pollution, and to treat illness with medicines that work in count with the body's own defense. Plant derived products can be exploited with sustainable, comparative and competitive advantage. These include reduced cost, less dangerous, more effective and readily available [14]. Tribal healers in most of the countries, frequently use herbal medicine to treat cut wounds, skin infection, swelling, aging, eczema and gastric ulcer [15]. The different parts of plants used for skin diseases contain some active principles or components that are antimicrobial and nutritive in function [16]. Medicinal plants have been used in traditional treatment of skin diseases worldwide. *AcaIypha wilkesiana* is a common ornamental plant in southern Nigeria used as a herbal remedy for the treatment of undefined skin infections in children [17]. Iranian traditional medicine (ITM), uses plants in the treatment of burns, dermatophytes and infectious diseases or as an antiseptic and anti-inflammatory agents [18]. Plants and its phytoconstituents are used to treat fungal infections particularly candidiasis such as oropharyngeal candidiasis, vulvovaginal candidiasis and others such as spirotrichosis, chromoblastomycosis, etc. [19]. South African plant *Dodonaea vuscosa* Var. angustifolia, leaves and twigs extracts is traditionally used as a gargle for oral candidiasis [20]. Septilin, an Ayurvedic herbal formulation, is used extensively as an immunomodulator and has also been employed in the treatment of various skin infections [21]. Benjamen et al. [22] and Abatan [23] reported that leaf juice and decoctions of *Senna alata* are used in the treatment of ringworm and other skin diseases. Other herbs known to be used for treatment of skin infections include *Quisqualis indica*, *Cormelina benghalensis, Amaranthus spinosus, Ramunculus scleratus, Cassia alata* [24]. In search for novel leads from herbal drugs against stubborn skin diseases caused by microorganisms some plants which are traditionally claimed to be used in the treatment of skin diseases were screened for their potential as antimicrobial agents. The plants screened for antibacterial and antifungal activity are *Asteracantha longifolia, Curcuma amada, Curcuma longa, Daemia extensa, Euphorbia hirta, Euphorbia tirucalli, Euphorbia nerrifolia, Heliotropium indicum, Morus alba, Pithecellobium dulce* and *Trichedesma indicum.*

CHAPTER IV

Skin disease is a common ailment. Skin complaints affects all ages from the neonate to the elderly and cause harm in number of ways.

Surveys suggest that approximately 1 to 7 in 10 of all visits to a primary care physician is for a skin problem and that for many hospitals the number of patients attending for dermatological diagnosis and treatment exceeds the total number of visits for the whole of medicine.

Population prevalence studies are in keeping with these figures, revealing an enormous burden of undiagnosed, untreated skin disease.

The management process depends upon the chronicity of the illness, investigations done to identify the disease, and the appropriate medications given.

The skin serves many functions particularly: protection, thermoregulation, percutaneaous absorption, secretory, and sensory. It has been estimated that skin diseases account for 34% of all occupational diseases.

In a study it was revealed that skin diseases constituted 6.3% of the total number of the patients who attended medical care .

The management of skin diseases is becoming a priority due to the association of skin opportunistic infections and HIV/AIDS. Estimates show that 92% of HIVinfected individuals have cuteneous and mucosal complications.

Infectious diseases, particularly skin and mucosal infections, are common in most of the tribal inhabitants due to lack of sanitation, potable water and awareness of hygienic food habits .

An important group of these skin pathogens are the fungi, among which dermatophytes and *Candida* spp., besides certain pathogenic bacteria are the most frequent .

Furthermore, in the last few years, the numbers of immune-suppressed and immune compromised patients, who frequently develop opportunistic systemic and superficial mycoses such as candidiasis, dermato-mycosis, fungal infections etc., have increased dramatically.

This is mainly due to the non-availability of effective antifungal drugs for systemic fungal infections and toxicity of available drugs like amphotericin-B Thus there is an increased need for the development of alternative antipathogenic substances.

One possible approach is to screen local medicinal plants in search of suitable chemotherapeutic antibacterial and antifungal substances. The herbalists prescribed various preparations of medicinal plants in treating ailments such as itch, eczema, scabies and skin diseases .

Traditional medicinal resources, especially plants, have been found to play a major role in managing dermatological conditions .

The demand for herbal medicines is increasing rapidly due to their lack of side effects. Further as health care costs continue to escalate, the attraction for low-cost remedies has stimulated consumers to re-evaluate the potential of alternatives .

According to WHO, herbal medicines serve the health needs of about 80% of the world's population, especially for millions of people in the vast rural areas of developing countries. In Ethiopia, traditional remedies represent not only part of the struggle of the people to fulfill their essential drug needs but also they are integral components of the cultural beliefs and attitudes .

More than 95% of traditional 13 preparations in different countries are of plant origin . Some of the common uses of the medicinal plants sold in markets include fumigation, vermifuge, pain relief and treating skin infections.

Antimicrobial and wound healing plants are among some of the major medicinal plants that are commonly available in markets. Plantderived products of different therapeutic categories of pharmaceutical preparations are currently recommended by medical practitioners and they form an important part of the health-care system in the modern world .

CHAPTER V

1. *Abrus precatorius* Fabaceae
2. *Achyranthes aspera* Amaranthaceae
3. *Acorus calamus* Araceae
4. *Aloe vera* Liliaceae
5. *Anisomeles indica* Lamiaceae
6. *Aristolochia bracteolate* Aristolochaceae
7. *Bauhinia vahlii* Caesalpiniaceae
8. *Bauhinia variegate* Caesalpiniaceae
9. *Blumea lacera* Asteraceae
10. *Buchanania cochinchinensis* Anacardiaceae
11. *Calatropis gigantean* Asclepiadaceae
12. *Cannabis sativa* Cannabinaceae
13. *Chenopodium album* Chenopodiacea
14. *Cinnamomum camphora* Lauraceae
15. *Citrullus colocynthis* Cucurbitaceae
16. *Curcuma domesticata*Zingiberaceae
17. *Erythrina variegate* Fabaceae
18. *Eugenia uniflora* Myrtaceae
19. *Ficus racemosa* Moraceae
20. *Glycyrrhiza glabra* Fabaceae
21. *Gmelina asiatica* Verbenaceae
22. *Holarrhena antidysenterica* Apocynaceae
23. *Hypericum calycinum* Hypericaceae
24. *Jatropha gossypifolia* Euphorbiaceae
25. *Luffa cylindrical* Cucurbitaceae
26. *Lygodium flexulosum* Lycopodiaceae
27. *Mimosa pudica* Mimosaceae
28. *Ocimum basilicum* Lamiaceae
29. *Ocimum sanctum*Lamiaceae
30. *Plumbago zeylanica* Plumbaginaceae
31. *Polygonum bistorta* Polygonaceae
32. *Rheum emodi* Polygonaceae
33. *Rubus fruticosus* Rosaceae

34. *Salvia officinalis* Labiateae
35. *Sida acuta* Malvaceae
36. *Sphaeranthus indicus* Compositae
37. *Syzygium cumini* Myrtaceae
38. *Tinospora cordifolia* Menispermaceae
39. *Typha elephantine* Typhaceae
40. *Verbascum sinaiticum* Scrophulariaceae
41. *Vitex altissima* Verbenaceae
42. *Zingiber officinale* Zingiberaceae

CHAPTER VI

ALANGIUM SALVIFOLIUM
B.S : ALANGIUM SALVIFOLIUM
Family : Cornaceae
Vernacular Name:
Eng name : Sage leaved Alangium
Hindi : Angol,Dhera,
Malayalam : Ankolam,Velithondi
Telugu : Urgu
Tamil : Alandi
PLANT DESCRIPTION
A small, thorny deciduous tree/ shrub which grows up to a height of 5-10 meters. Bark yellowish, leaves alternate, elliptical and usually unequal at the base; flowers-yellowish white, fragrant, in axillary fascicles,fruits 1-2 seeded,1cm in length,1-2 seeded berries crowned by the calyx lobes.
Action : Alterative, anthelmintic, febrifuge
Chemical constituents: Alangine.
Uses in Siddha :

- The stem bark is powdered and is sprayed externally for leprosy, scabies, etc.

- The medicated oil prepared is used externally and internally with palm jaggery for scabies, gonorrheal and syphilitic ulcers

- The oil prepared from its seed is used internally with palm jaggery for leprosy

CHAPTER VII

2.1.2 ARISTOLOCHIA BRACTEOLATA

B.S : Aristolochia bracteolate

Family : Aristolochiaceae

Vernacular Nammes

Eng name :Indian birthwort; worm killer

Gujarati: Kidamari

Marathi: Gnadhan, Gandhati

Bengali: Taamaak

Kannada: Karigid, Kattagiri,

Tamil: Adutinnalai

Telugu: Gadidegadapara

Malayalam: Adutinnapali

Action : Anthelmintic, alterative, stimulant , tonic

Chemical constituents: Glucosides, isoaristolochic acis, Allantoin and isovanillin are obtained from this plant.

Uses in Siddha

- The decoction of the leaves is used to cure dermatitis, and various types of rashes, in common .
- The juice of the plant is mixed with gingelly oil and is heated. This oil is used for dermatitis , and other allergic disorders. And when given internally for 40 days cures the lesions of leprosy.

CHAPTER VIII

DATURA METEL
   B.S : Datura metel
   Family : Solanaceae
   Vernacular Names
   Eng name : Thorn apple
   Sanskrit Name : Dhatura
   Hindi Name : Dhatura
   Action : Vermicide, anti-spasmodic, anodyne
   Chemical constituents : Hyoscine, Hyoscyamine, Atropine
   Uses in Siddha

- The oil prepared from its leaf is used for diabetic ulcer, chronic ulcers, and cut wounds and other extra growths.
- The fruit of the plant is made dry and is powdered and is applied externally for scabies, allergic dermatitis.

CHAPTER IX

2.1.4 GLORIOSA SUPERBA

B.S : Gloriosa superb

Family : Liliaceae

Vernacular Name

Eng name : Malabar glory lily

Sanskirt : Langli, Visalya

Hindi :Karihari Languli

Kannada :Agnishike, Gowrihoo,Akkatangiballi

Tamil :Nabhikkodi

Action : Alterative, anti-periodic, purgative

Constituents : Gloriosine, Superbine

Uses in Siddha

The root tuber is mixed with babchi seeds(Psoralea corylifoila) , black cumin(Nigella sativa) and purple fleebane(Vernonia anthelmintica) and is made to a paste and is applied externally for various skin diseases.

CHAPTER X

2.1.5 INDIGOFERA ASPALATHOIDES

B.S : Indigofera asplathoides

Family : Papilionaceae

Vernacular Name

Eng name : Indigo plant

Sanskrit Name : Ranjani

English Name : Indigo

Kannada Name : Nili

Hindi Name :Nili

Action : Stimulant, demulcent

Constituents : Specific oil, dyes

Uses in Siddha

• The decoction of the leaves and flowers is used for various types of rashes in skin.

• The root is used in preparing medicated oil and is applied externally for scabies, leprosy etc.

• The medicated oil prepared from its root is given internally with the powder of the whole plant for leprosy, dermatitis, and various ulcers.

CHAPTER XI

2.1.6 SEMECARPUS ANACARDIUM

B.S : Semecarpus anacardium

Family : Anacardiaceae

Vernacular Name

Eng name : Marking nut tree

Malayalam : Thenkotta,

Sanskrit : Agni mukhi,

Hindi : Bhilava, Bhilawa

Tamil : Tatamkottai, Scramkotati, Sen kottai

Kannada : Bhallataka,

Telugu : Jeedi vithullu

Konkani : Amberi

Action : Alterative, caustic

Chemical constituents: Anacardic acid, Cardol, Anacardol, Semecarpol.

Uses in Siddha :

The nut is purified and is processed in several forms such as powder,oil, ghee, and leghyam and is given for various skin disease like leucoderma, allergic dermatitis, poisonous bites leprosy etc.

CHAPTER XII

2.1.7 HYDNOCARPUS LAURIFOLIA

B.S: Hydnocarpus laurifolia

Family: Flacourtiaceae

Vernacular Name:

Sanskrit Name : Tuvaraka

Kannada Name : Suranti, surti, toratti

Hindi Name : Chaulmoogra

Eng name : Jangli almond, Chaulmugra

Action : Parasiticide, alterative, detergent, stimulant

Chemical constituents: Chaulmoogric acid, Hydnocarpic acid

Uses in Siddha

• The kennel is soaked in lemon juice or curd and is made into a paste and is applied externally for itching, scabies.

• The medicated oil obtained from its seed is used for leprosy, hyper vitaminosis A (Phrenoderma)

CHAPTER XIII

2.1.8 SMILAX CHINA

B.S : Smilax china

Family : Liliaceae

Vernacular Name

Eng name : China root

Hindi : Chopchini

Malayalam : Pavu, Cheenapavu

PLANT DESCRIPTION

A hard tendril climber with prickles all over the stem. Leaves simple, alternate, elliptic, acute and sometimes obtuse and nerved, with prominent stipule at base of leaves. Flowers, white, small and many, found in axillary umbels. Fruits red globose berries. Rhizomes are long, thick and grey colored. Cut surfaces yellowish white colored.

Action : Anti-syphilitic, alterative,

Chemical constituents : Fat, Glucoside, Saponin, Gum, Starch.

Uses in Siddha

The root tuber is prepared in various forms like powder, medicated oil, decoction and is used for various skin diseases like dermatitis, ulcers, scabies ,leucoderma etc.

CHAPTER XIV

2.1.9 WRIGHTIA TINCTORIA

B.S : Wrightia tinctoria

Family : Apocyanaceae

Vernacular Name

Eng name : Pala indigo plant

Hindi :Indarjou

Malayalam : Dhantappala

Sanskrit :Kutajah

Tamil : Nilappalai

Action : Astringent, tonic, anthelmintic

Chemical constituents: Glucoside, and certain alkaloids.

Uses in Siddha

The leaf is soaked in coconut oil and is kept in hot sun for a day and the oil obtained is used for psoriasis and this is proven clinically.

CHAPTER XV

Gloriosa superba

    B.S : Gloriosa superb

    Family : Liliaceae

    Vernacular Name

    English : Malabar glory lily

    Sanskirt : Langli, Visalya

    Hindi :Karihari Languli

    Kannada :Agnishike, Gowrihoo,Akkatangiballi

    Tamil :Nabhikkodi

    Action : Alterative, anti-periodic, purgative

    Constituents : Gloriosine, Superbine

Uses in Siddha :The root tuber is mixed with babchi seeds (Psoralea corylifoila) , black cumin(Nigella sativa) and purple fleebane(Vernonia anthelmintica) and is complete to a paste and is applied outwardly for various skin diseases.

INDIGOFERA ASPALATHOIDES
    B.S : Indigofera asplathoides
    Family : Papilionaceae
    Vernacular Name
    Eng : Indigo plant
    Sanskrit : Ranjani
    English : Indigo
    Kannada : Nili
    Hindi :Nili
    Action : Stimulant, demulcent
    Constituents : Specific oil, dyes
    Uses in Siddha

• The decoction of the leaves and flowers is used for various types of rashes in skin.

• The root is used in preparing medicated oil and is applied externally for scabies, leprosy etc.

• The medicated oil prepared from its root is given internally with the fine particles of the whole plant for leprosy, dermatitis, and a variety of ulcers.

CHAPTER XVII

Semecarpus anacardium

B.S : *Semecarpus anacardium*

Family : Anacardiaceae

Vernacular Name

Eng name : Marking nut tree

Malayalam : Thenkotta,

Sanskrit : Agni mukhi,

Hindi : Bhilava, Bhilawa

Tamil : Tatamkottai, Scramkotati, Sen kottai

Kannada : Bhallataka,

Telugu : Jeedi vithullu

Konkani : Amberi

Action : Alterative, caustic

Chemical constituents: Anacardic acid, Cardol, Anacardol, Semecarpol.

Uses in Siddha : The nut is purified and is processed in a number of forms such as powder, oil, ghee, and leghyam and is given for a range of skin disease like leucoderma, allergic dermatitis, toxic bites leprosy etc.

CHAPTER XVIII

Hydnocarpus laurifolia
    B.S: Hydnocarpus laurifolia
    Family: Flacourtiaceae
    Vernacular Name:
    Sanskrit : Tuvaraka
    Kannada : Suranti, surti, toratti
    Hindi : Chaulmoogra
    Eng : Jangli almond, Chaulmugra
    Action : Parasiticide, alterative, detergent, stimulant
    Chemical constituents: Chaulmoogric acid, Hydnocarpic acid
    Uses in Siddha

• The kennel is covered with water in lemon juice or curd and is made into a paste and is applied externally for itching, scabies. The medicated oil obtained from its seed is used for leprosy, hyper vitaminosis A (Phrenoderma)

CHAPTER XIX

Smilax china

B.S : Smilax china

Family : Liliaceae

Vernacular Name

Eng name : China root

Hindi : Chopchini

Malayalam : Pavu, Cheenapavu

PLANT DESCRIPTION: A hard tendril climber with prickles all in surplus of the stem. Leaves simple, alternate, elliptic, acute and sometimes obtuse and nerved, with prominent stipule at base of leaves. Flowers, white, small and many, found in axillary umbels. Fruits red globose berries. Rhizomes are long, thick and grey colored. Cut surfaces yellowish white colored.

Action : Anti-syphilitic, alterative,

Chemical constituents: Fat, Glucoside, Saponin, Gum, Starch.

Uses in Siddha : The root tuber is prepared in a variety of forms like powder, medicated oil, decoction and is used for various skin diseases like dermatitis, ulcers, scabies ,leucoderma etc.

WRIGHTIA TINCTORIA

B.S : *Wrightia tinctoria*

Family : Apocyanaceae

Vernacular Name

English : Pala indigo plant

Hindi :Indarjou

Malayalam : Dhantappala

Sanskrit :Kutajah

Tamil : Nilappalai

Action : Astringent, tonic, anthelmintic

Chemical constituents: Glucoside, and certain alkaloids.

Uses in Siddha

The leaf is soaked in coconut oil and is reserved in hot sun for a day and the oil obtained is used for psoriasis and this is established clinically.

Conclusion:

In progress world-wide attention in traditional medicine has lead to fast growth and studies of numerous remedies working by a diversity of racial groups of the globe. There are numerals of medicinal plants which are used traditionally by the tribal people in skin disorder. In attention of the study we recognized number of medicinal plants used by the people to cure dermatological disorders. More wide ethno-botanical and ethno-pharmacological study may show the way to the growth of medicinal plants for skin care and heal. Thus, the major aim of the current review is to discover and scheme the medicinal plants which have the probable to become the modern drug alternate for skin disorder.

CHAPTER XXI

References

REFERENCES:

1. Kohen R. Skin antioxidants: Their role in aging and in oxidative stress-New approaches for their evaluation. *Biomedicine and Pharmacotherapy.* 1999;53:181-192.

2. Desta B. Ethiopian traditional herbal drugs. Part II: Antimicrobial activity of 63 medicinal plants. *Journal of Ethnopharmacology.* 1993;39:129-139.

3. Jawetz E, Janet S, Nicholas L, Edwards E. Skin microorganisms. In: *Medical Microbiology.* Lange International, NY; 1978:25-27.

4. Robert C, Kupper TS. Inflammatory skin diseases, T cells and immune surveillance. *New England Journal of Medicine.*1999; 341:1817-1828.

5. Madigan MT, Martinko JM, Parker J. *Brock Biology of Microorganisms.* 10th ed. Pearson Education, London; 2003.

6. Lory S. Pseudomonas and other nonfermenting Bacilli. In: Davis BD, Dulbecco R, Eisen HN, Ginsberg HS, eds. *Microbiology*, 4th ed. Lippincott Co, Philadelphia; 1990:595-600.

7. Murray PR, Drew WL, Kobayashi GS, Thompson JH. *Medical Microbiology.* Mosby Co, Philadelphia; 1990:119-126.

8. Aleman CT, Wallace ML, Blaylock WK, Garrett AB. Subcutaneous nodules caused by *Pseudomonas aeruginosa* without sepsis.*Cutis.* 1999;63:161-163.

9. Latha PS, Kannabiran K. Antimicrobial activity and phytochemicals of *Solanum trilobatum* Linn. *African Journal of Biotechnology.* 2006;5:2402-2404.

10. Chah KF, Eze CA, Emuelosi CE, Esimone CO. Antibacterial and wound healing properties of methanolic extracts of some Nigerian medicinal plants. *Journal of Ethnopharmacology.* 2006;104: 164-167.

11. Nair R, Kalariya T, Chanda S. Antibacterial activity of some selected Indian medicinal flora. *Turkish Journal of Biology.*2005;29:41-47.

12. Parekh J, Chanda S. *In vitro* antibacterial activity of the crude methanol extract of *Woodfordia fructicosa* Kurz. Flower (Lythraceae). *Brazilian Journal of Microbiology.* 2007a;38:204-207.

13. Al-Bakri AG, Afifi FU. Evaluation of antimicrobial activity of selected plant extracts by rapid XTT colorimetry and bacterial enumeration. *Journal of Microbiological Methods.* 2007;68:19-25.

14. Moorthy K, Srinivasan K, Subramanian C, Mohanasundari C, Palaniswamy M. Phytochemical screening and antibacterial evaluation of stem bark of *Mallotus philippinensis* var. tomentosus. *African Journal of Biotechnology.* 2007;6:1521-1523.

15. Samy RP, Ignacimuthu S, Sen A. Screening of 34 Indian medicinal plants for antibacterial properties. *Journal of Ethnopharmacology.* 1998;62:173-181.

16. Esimone CO, Ibezim EC, Chah KF. The wound healing effect of herbal ointments formulated with *Napoleona imperialis.Journal of Pharmaceutical and Allied Sciences.* 2005;3:294-299.

17. Alade PI, Irobi ON. Antimicrobial activities of crude leaf extracts of *Acalypha wilkesiana. Journal of Ethnopharmacology.*1993;39:171-174.

18. Ghahraman A, Attar F. *Biological Diversity of Iranian Plant Species.* Tehran Univ Press, Tehran; 1998:24-35.

19. Denning DW, Evans EGV, Kibbler CC, Richardson MD, Roberts MM, Rogers TR, Warnock DW, Warren RE. Guidelines for the investigation of invasive fungal infections in haematological malignancy and solid organ transplantation. *European Journal of Clinical Microbiology and Infectious Diseases.* 1997;16:424-436.

20. Van Wyk BE, Van Oudtshoorn B, Gericke N. *Medicinal Plants of South Africa.* Briza Publications, Pretoria; 2002:108-109.

21. Rao CS, Raju C, Gopumadhavan S, Chauhan BL, Kulkarni RD, Mitra SK. Immunotherapeutic modification by an ayurvedic formulation Septilin. *Indian Journal of Experimental Biology.* 1994;32:553-558.

22. Benjamin TV, Lamikanra A. Investigation of *Cassia alata,* a plant used in Nigeria in the treatment of skin diseases.*Pharmaceutical Biology.* 1981;19:93-96.

23. Abatan MO. A note on the anti-inflammatory action of plants of some Cassia species. *Fitoterapia.* 1990; 61:336-338.

24. Damodaran S, Venkataraman S. A study on the therapeutic efficacy of *Cassia alata,* Linn. leaf extract against Pityriasis versicolor. *Journal of Ethnopharmacology.* 1994;42:19-23.

25. Siddha Materia Medica (Medicinal Plants Division) by Murugesa Mudaliar, Published by The Directorate of Indian Medicine & Homeopathy, Chennai.

26. Indian Materia Medica Vol: 1 by, Dr. K.M. Nadkarani, Publisher: Popular Prakash, Mumbai.
27. Formulary of Siddha Medicines (Siddha Vaithiya Thirattu . in Tamil) by Dr. K.N. Kuppusamy Muthaliar and Dr. K.S. Uthamarayan, Published by Indian Medicine and Homeopathy Department, Chennai . 600 106, India.

Conclusion:

In progress world-wide attention in traditional medicine has lead to fast growth and studies of numerous remedies working by a diversity of racial groups of the globe. There are numerals of medicinal plants which are used traditionally by the tribal people in skin disorder. In attention of the study we recognized number of medicinal plants used by the people to cure dermatological disorders. More wide ethno-botanical and ethno-pharmacological study may show the way to the growth of medicinal plants for skin care and heal. Thus, the major aim of the current review is to discover and scheme the medicinal plants which have the probable to become the modern drug alternate for skin disorder.

www.ingramcontent.com/pod-product-compliance
Lightning Source LLC
Chambersburg PA
CBHW060220170726
48004CB00014B/875